Awakening Series

Smile

PUBLISHED BY:

Take Abreak

Take Abreak organized a blessing ceremony to fundraise for victims of earthquake. After that event, Take Abreak founded a line group to encourage participants to keep on the meditation shared on the blessing ceremony.

Take Abreak has been sharing a piece of article with group members since then. That's the beginning of this Awakening Series.

1.

We smile

Then the world shines as well.

We become walking suns.

We make ourselves warm.

We also make every corner we go warm.

2.

All people and all things we project are all

from our thoughts.

When we treat them with a smile,

the frequency our smile vibrates will bring

us warmth and abundance.

Bless you.

3.

We read a lot of classics and learn a lot of

skillful means.

But if we do not contemplate our hearts and

do not lay down our false self,

we can not see our true selves which are full

of divinity, compassion and joy.

You can not decide whether your quantum

entanglement is at the upper string or the

lower string.

But you are a great creator.

Smile and be mindful.

They will bring us into the world we create.

4.

We die in every second yet we also reborn

in every second.

Every beautiful fragment is like the

circulation of life.

It looks like a beautiful continuation in this

linear time and space.

The only unchanged part in this universe is

that it changes all the time.

Others are us.

We do for ourselves and at the same time we

also do for others.

Thank you for making the world better.

5.

We define what happy is and what pain is.

Then we choose a motivation through this

kind of belief.

Our body will automatically operate based

on the motivation we choose.

When we are peaceful in awareness state,

we would smile by the light of nature.

Then we are going to define what

benevolence is and to choose this

benevolence.

We will tune ourselves in the frequency of

smile.

And everything corresponding with us will

come because of us.

6.

Face our dark side with smile.

Accept the situation that we still can not

accept a certain thing.

This process is also a turning point to

transform ourselves.

Each pain is an opportunity.

There is no need to think or judge with brain.

We can just tell ourselves with a smile:

I accept the situation that I still can not

accept this thing.

7.

The light in our nature makes everything

awaken.

The light in our nature also combines with

gunas and makes everything look like the

life we know.

But if we pull ourselves away from this

natural awakening, everything will go back

to illusion again.

Since we are cultivating a true nature in this

illusion, we can smile at any situation.

8.

We are all gardeners of our soul and spirit.

We decide when to plow, what to weed or

what to sow.

We are plowing our spiritual pure land with

smile in the glowing sun.

9.

If all beings and I all fear nothing, how

could there be no smile.

10.

All seeds of karma would blossom and bear

fruits one day due to our good deeds or bad

deeds.

We smile at the consequences from all the

causes.

We accept them without reaction.

This is the effort what our spiritual

cultivation gives us.

11.

Often we already gain rewards of abundant

joy just at the moment we give out our smile.

Sometimes at the moment we are developing

our smile,

even at the moment we are just developing

or learning to give out smiles, we have

gained whole-hearted joy.

12.

Be grateful to all the abundance in our life.

And give others abundance with smile. We

can then feel that all energies are wonderful.

13.

In this perverted world,

giving is actually attaining.

Giving or not giving are both spiritual

cultivations.

Experience the truth that every good time or

hard time is a gift from heaven with a smile.

14.

When we walk in tranquil and silence, we will smile at everyone.

Love flows naturally.

This is a feeling beyond secular point of view.

And this begins from breathing.

15.

Smile can vibrate our every cell and turn on

the chakras which used to be sleeping or

unbalanced.

It can help us see what lesson we should

learn.

Smile also helps us to accept the truth that

we reap what we grow under the rule of

karma.

It allows us to be our true selves and it

allows us to accept the truth

that we still can not accept a certain issues.

Smile makes us surrender to the constant

flow (which doesn't mean just go with the

flow but surrender with consciousness).

Smile makes us back to Oneness.

At that moment, you can understand why

you are actually everyone and everything

you give out is devoting to yourself.

16.

There is no need for us to judge things. All things are neutral.

Our perspectives and emotions are all from the idea of "me".

It is hard for us to take the panoramic view of the whole situation from height without understanding the cause and effect relationship.

There is not merely one cause.

And the effects can be multiple.

Look at all happenings with an aware and

compassionate heart.

At this time and space you are in, all

happenings are related to you.

This is not accidental.

We come here to experience and learn how

to transform ourselves and be aware of who

we are.

Just breathe, smile and be thankful.

17.

With our sincerity,

we bring out our nature with wisdom. Just

follow our virtues and cherish them with

smile and peace.

Unite with universe and earth.

18.

Close yours eyes,

open your heart and smile.

Back to Oneness.

When you open your eyes,

you'll discover that everything is yourself.

19.

Images, nouns, definitions, all these things

would melt in love. Warm energy would

surge in an endless stream.

It is infinite and boundless.

If we see from the surface of water, we can

see that although the water is contaminated,

its essence is very pure.

We look at the dark sides of all people and

things with smile.

Can we accept the so-called filth in our eyes

and make it a part of our life?

Can we stay away with wallowing in the

mire but use it as a mirror to contemplate

our inner heart?

20.

You are the creator of time, space and the

universe.

You project all these things in your belief.

And you get into it, into the limitation you

created.

You care about how much time has passed

and how many things you've accomplished.

You forget that an eternity an hour.

Actually time and space don't exist.

The reality you believe in is just like the

illusion explained in The Diamond Sutra.

No matter how tiny it is, a shooting moment

is eternity.

Then there won't be so-called birth and

death and thoughts.

But it doesn't mean that we don't have to do

anything since everything is just illusion and

emptiness.

Do not forget that all learning we experience, no matter it is about our body, spirit or personal relationship, they are all about karma. Through the mutual teaching and learning, we help ourselves and others.Our human body is precious. Let us support each other and make progress with smile and mindfulness.

Disclaimer

The information contained in this book is for general information purposes only. The information is provided by the authors and while we endeavor to keep the information up to date and correct, we make no representations or warranties of any kind, express or implied, about the completeness, accuracy, reliability, suitability or availability with respect to the book or the information, products, services, or related graphics contained in the book for any purpose. Any reliance you place on such information is therefore strictly at your own risk.